Monkey

1. Cover the tube with brown paper.
2. Color the monkey.
3. Cut out the monkey body pieces
   and paste them on the tube.

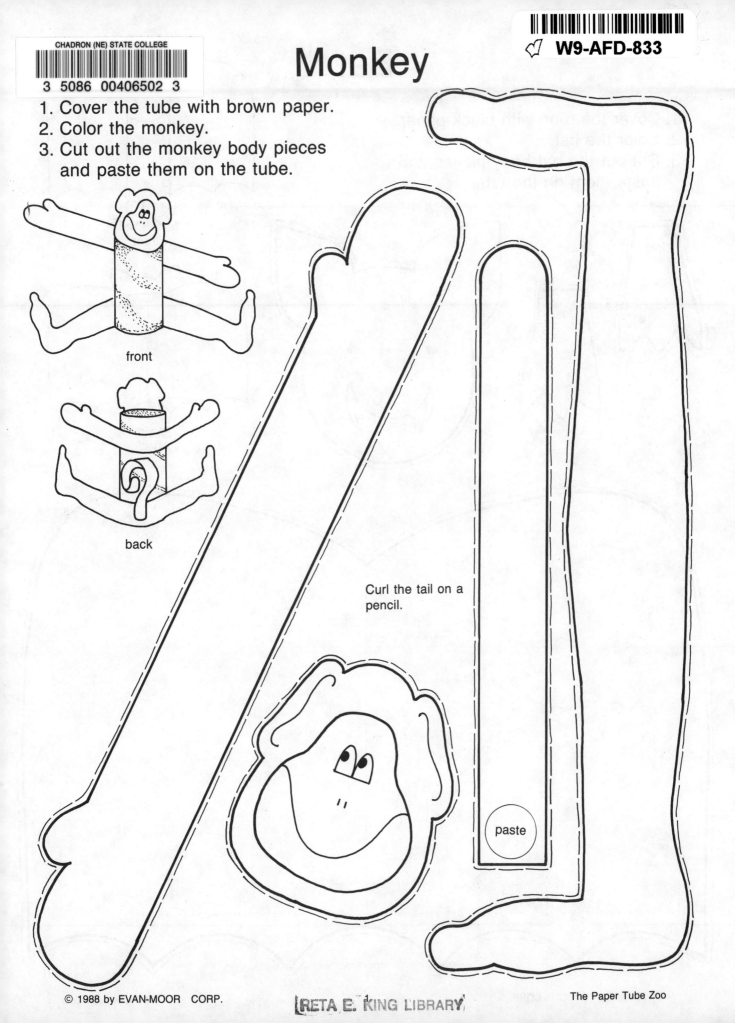

front

back

Curl the tail on a pencil.

paste

The Paper Tube Zoo

Bat

1. Cover the tube with black paper.
2. Color the bat.
3. Cut out the bat body pieces and paste them on the tube.

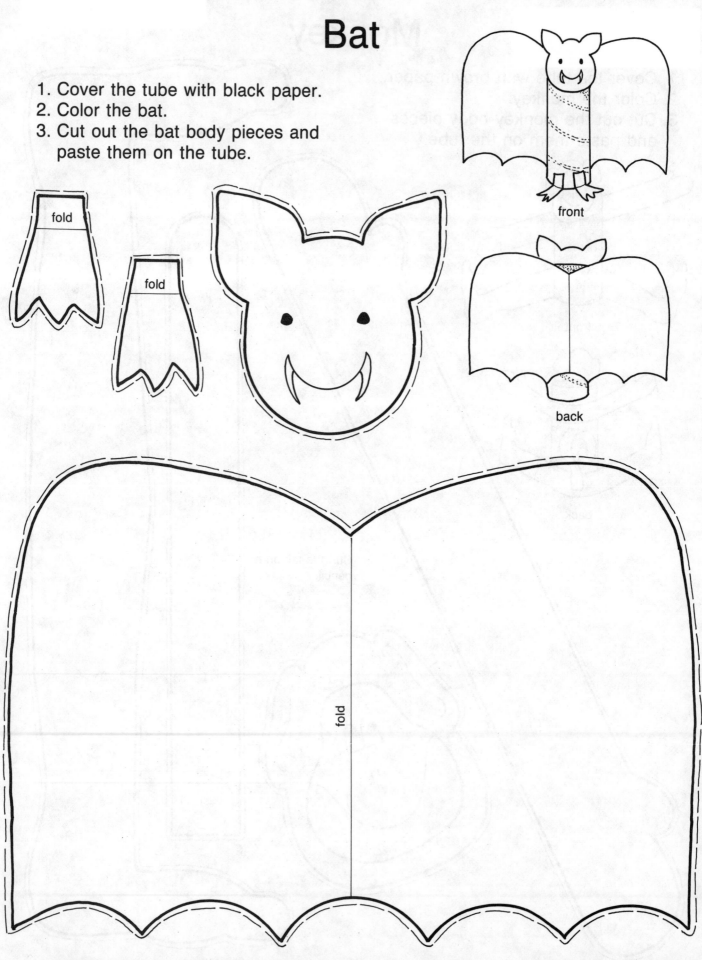

front

back

fold

fold

fold

Beaver

1. Cover the tube with brown paper.
2. Color the beaver.
3. Cut out the beaver body pieces and paste them on the tube.

side

back

fold

fold

cut

3

The Paper Tube Zoo

Bear

1. Cover the tube with brown paper.
2. Color the bear.
3. Cut out the bear body pieces and paste them on the tube.

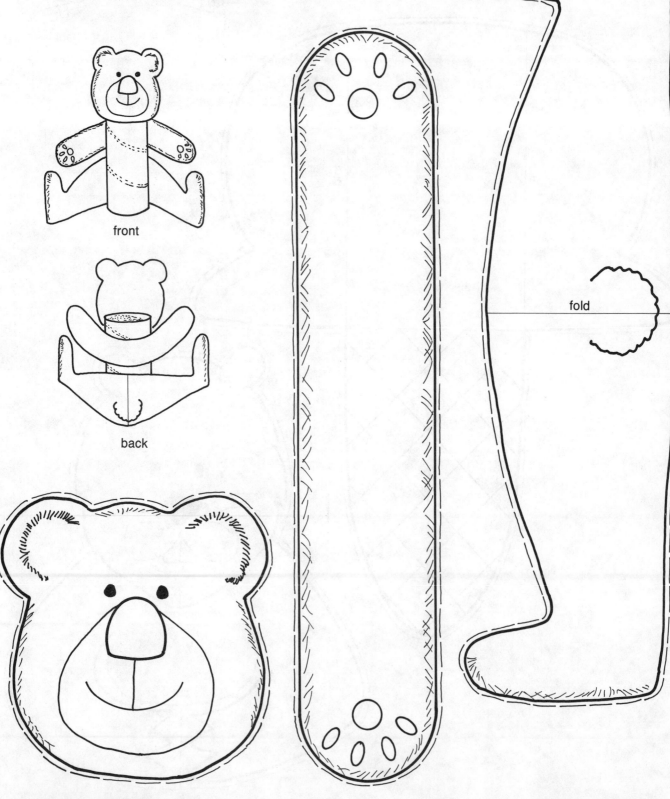

front

back

fold

Pig

1. Color the pig.
2. Cut out the pig body pieces and paste them on the tube.

front   back

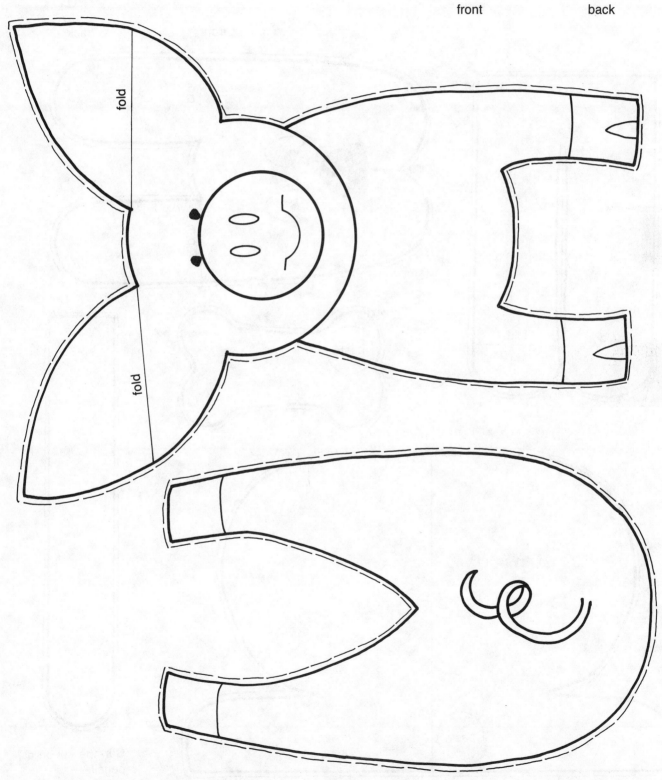

fold

fold

5

The Paper Tube Zoo

Dog

1. Cover the tube with paper.
2. Color the dog and his bone.
3. Cut out the dog body pieces and paste them on the tube.

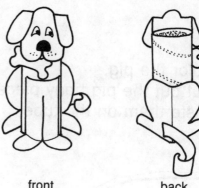

front   back

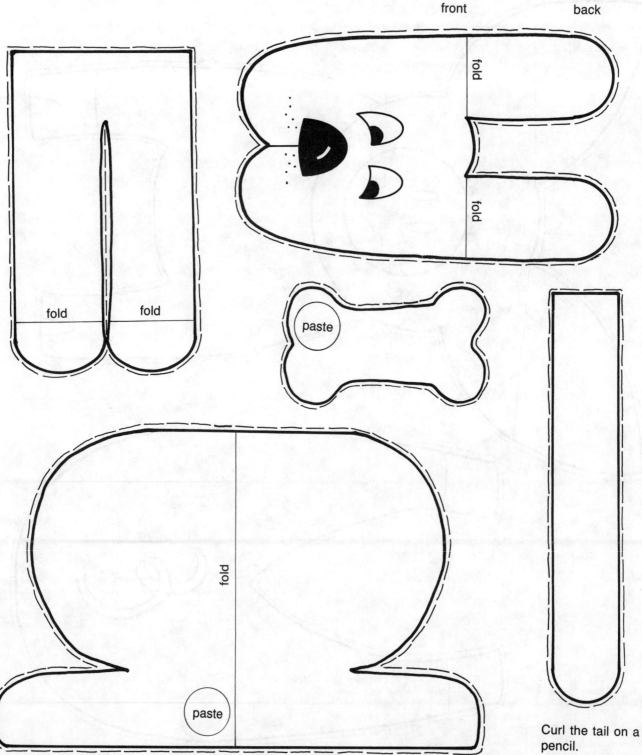

Curl the tail on a pencil.

6

The Paper Tube Zoo

Koala

1. Cover the tube with brown paper.
2. Color the koala.
3. Cut out the koala body pieces and paste them on the tube.

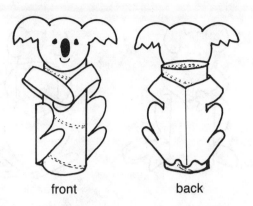

front   back

Wrap the arms around the tube.

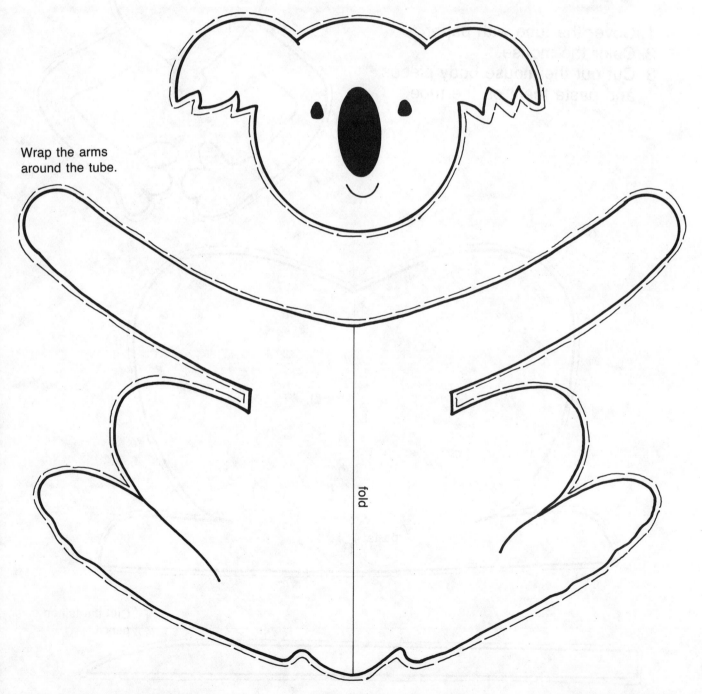

fold

     7   The Paper Tube Zoo

Mouse

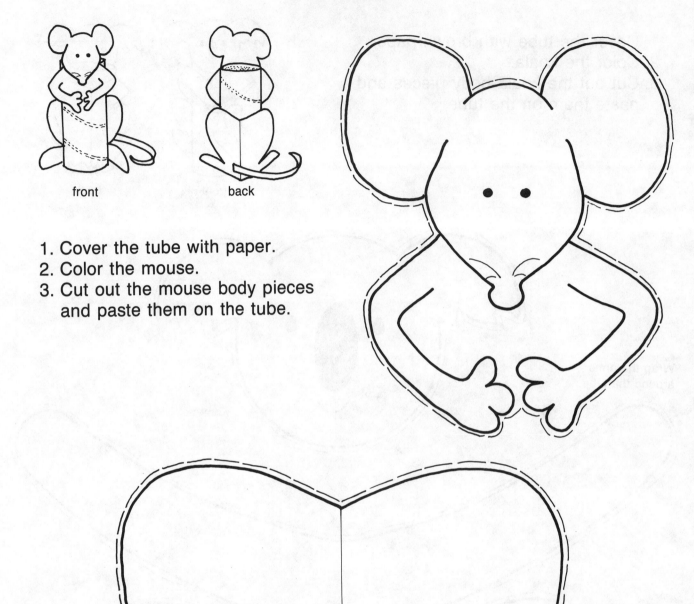

front

back

1. Cover the tube with paper.
2. Color the mouse.
3. Cut out the mouse body pieces and paste them on the tube.

fold

paste

Curl the tail on a pencil.

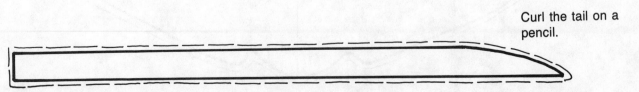

8

The Paper Tube Zoo

Duck

1. Cover the tube with paper.
2. Color the duck.
3. Cut out the duck body pieces and paste them on the tube.

wings

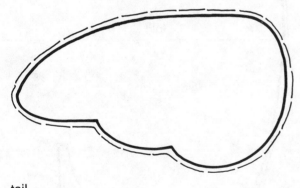

Paste wings on the side of the tube.

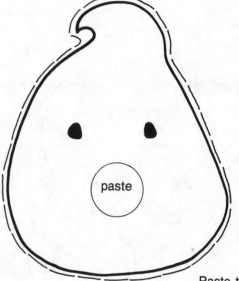

paste

Paste the beak on the duck's head.

tail

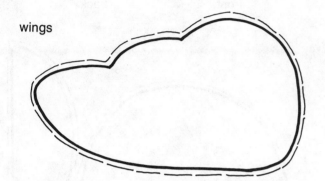

beak

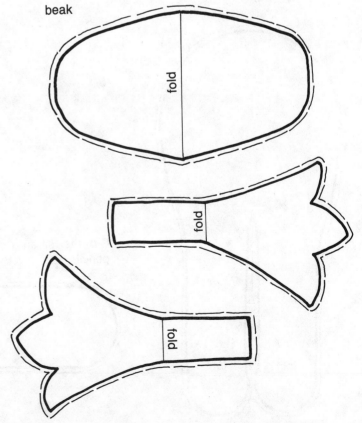

fold

fold

fold

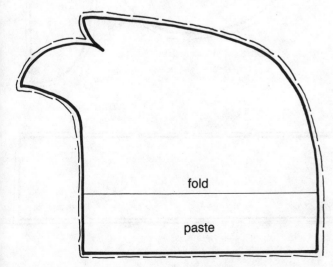

fold

paste

9

The Paper Tube Zoo

Cat

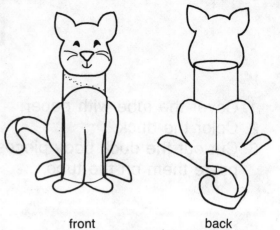

front   back

1. Cover the tube with paper.
2. Color the cat.
3. Cut out the cat body pieces and paste them on the tube.

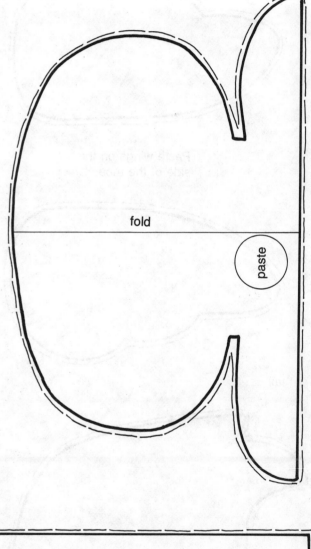

fold

paste

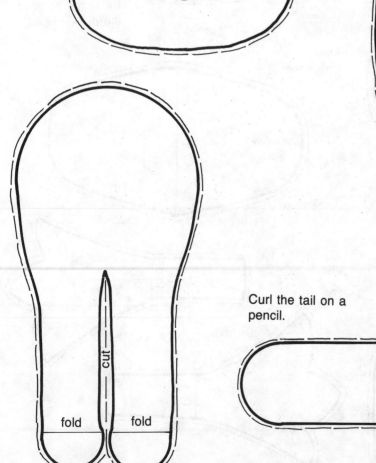

fold   cut   fold

Curl the tail on a pencil.

Cow

front   back

1. Cover the tube with brown paper.
2. Color the cow brown.
3. Cut out the cow body pieces and paste them on the tube.

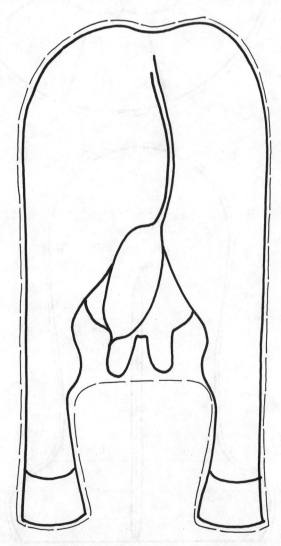

The Paper Tube Zoo

Lion

1. Cover the tube with yellow paper.
2. Color the lion.
3. Cut out the lion body pieces and
   paste them on the tube.

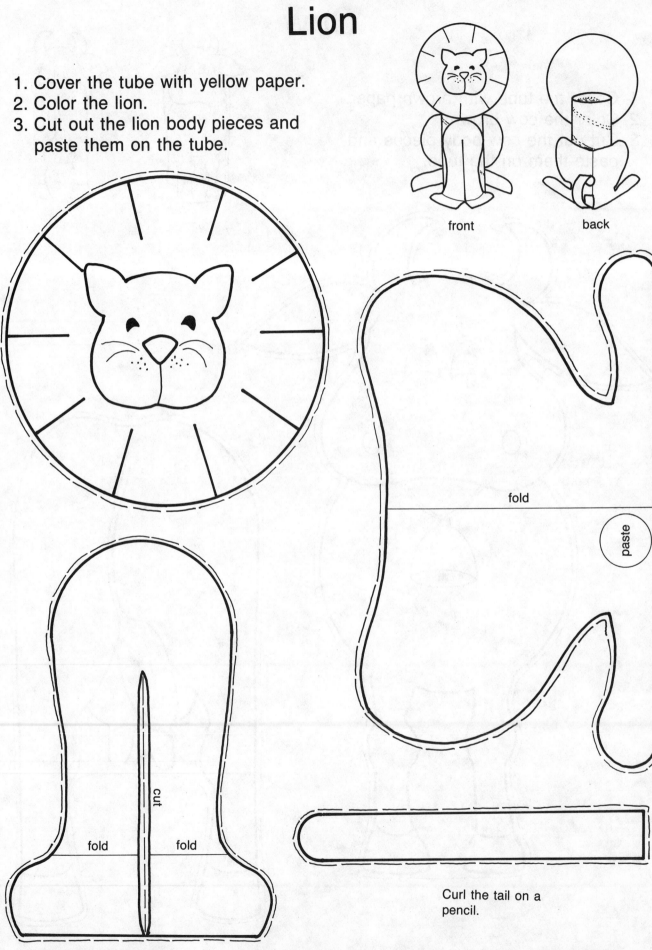

front

back

fold

paste

cut

fold   fold

Curl the tail on a
pencil.

12

Frog

1. Cover the tube with green paper.
2. Color the frog.
3. Cut out the frog body pieces and paste them on the tube.

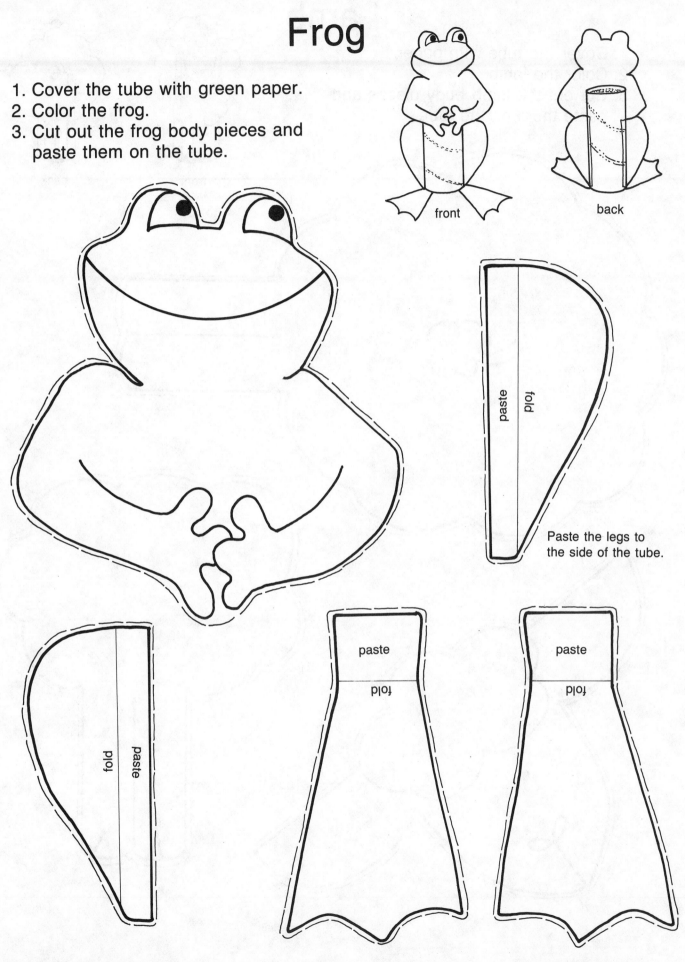

front

back

paste

fold

Paste the legs to the side of the tube.

fold

paste

paste

fold

paste

fold

13

The Paper Tube Zoo

Lamb

1. Cover the tube with paper.
2. Color the lamb.
3. Cut out the lamb body pieces and paste them on the tube.

front

back

14

The Paper Tube Zoo

Brontosaurus

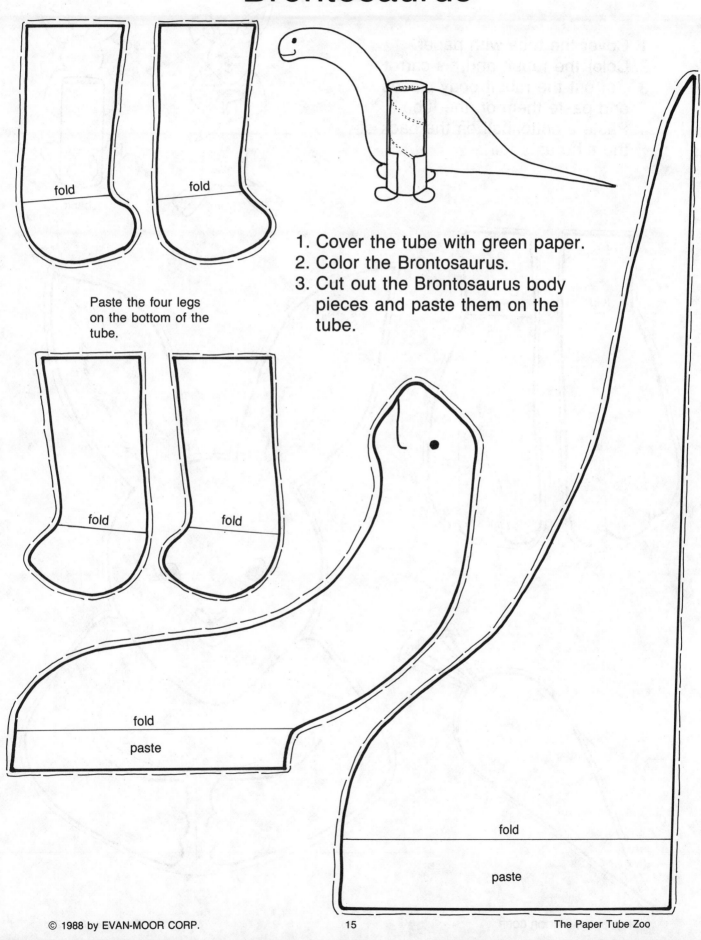

Paste the four legs on the bottom of the tube.

fold

fold

fold

fold

1. Cover the tube with green paper.
2. Color the Brontosaurus.
3. Cut out the Brontosaurus body pieces and paste them on the tube.

fold

paste

fold

paste

15

The Paper Tube Zoo

Bunny

1. Cover the tube with paper.
2. Color the rabbit and his carrot.
3. Cut out the rabbit body pieces and paste them on the tube.
4. Paste a cottonball on the back of the tube as a tail.

front   back

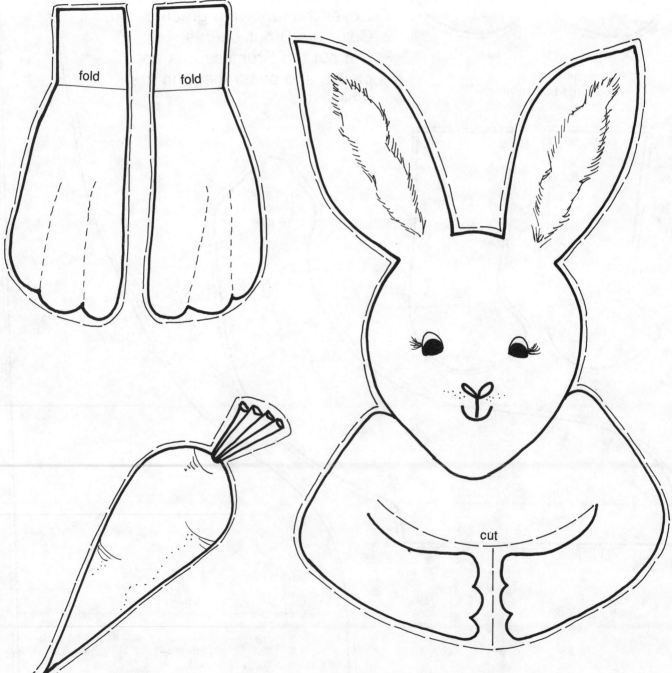

fold   fold

cut

16   The Paper Tube Zoo

Penguin

1. Cover the tube with black paper.
2. Color the penguin.
3. Cut out the penguin body pieces and paste them on the tube.

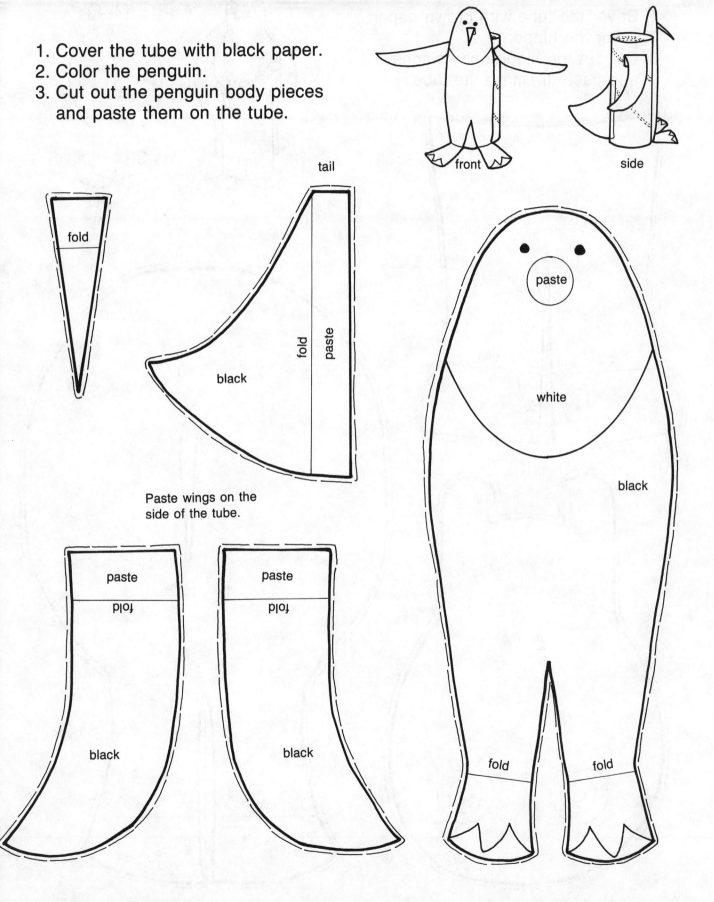

front

side

tail

fold

black

fold

paste

Paste wings on the side of the tube.

paste

white

black

paste

fold

paste

fold

black

black

fold

fold

17

The Paper Tube Zoo

Hippo

1. Cover the tube with brown paper.
2. Color the hippo.
3. Cut out the hippo body pieces and paste them on the tube.

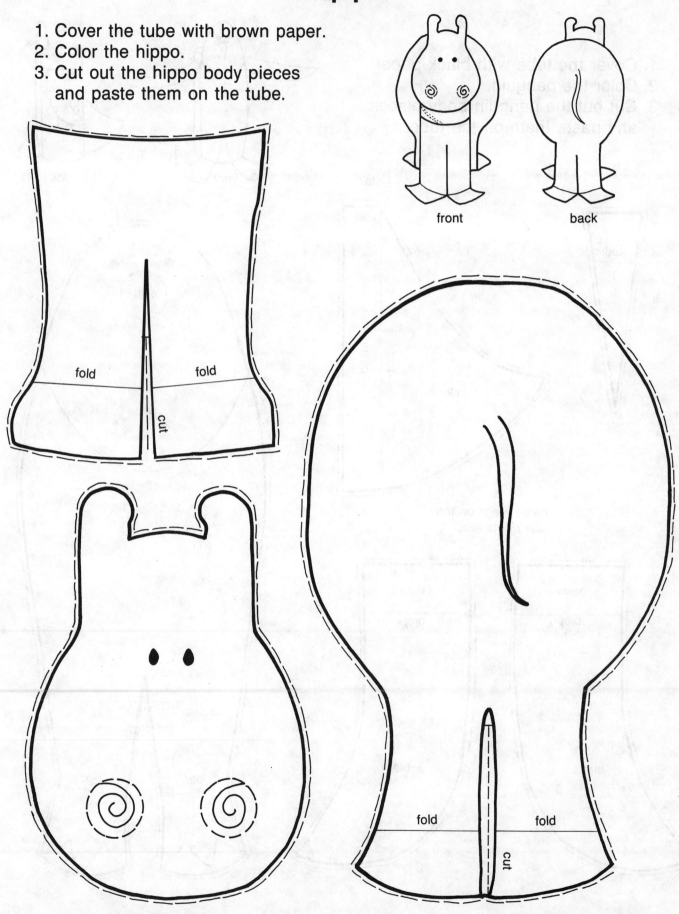

front

back

fold   fold

cut

fold   fold

cut

Toucan

1. Cover the tube with black paper.
2. Color the toucan.
3. Cut out the toucan body pieces and paste them on the tube.

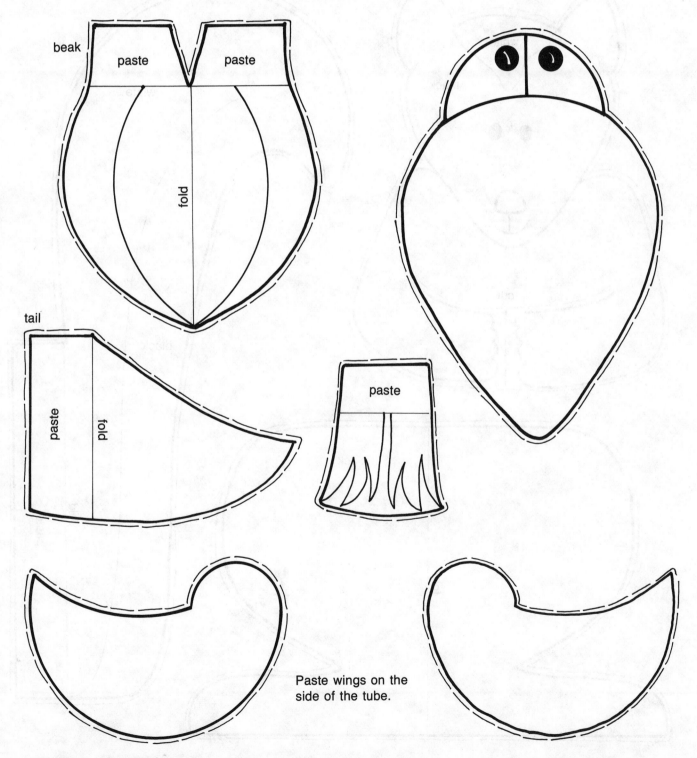

beak

paste   paste

fold

tail

paste   fold

paste

Paste wings on the side of the tube.

The Paper Tube Zoo

Skunk

1. Cover the tube with black paper.
2. Color the skunk.
3. Cut out the skunk body pieces and paste them on the tube.

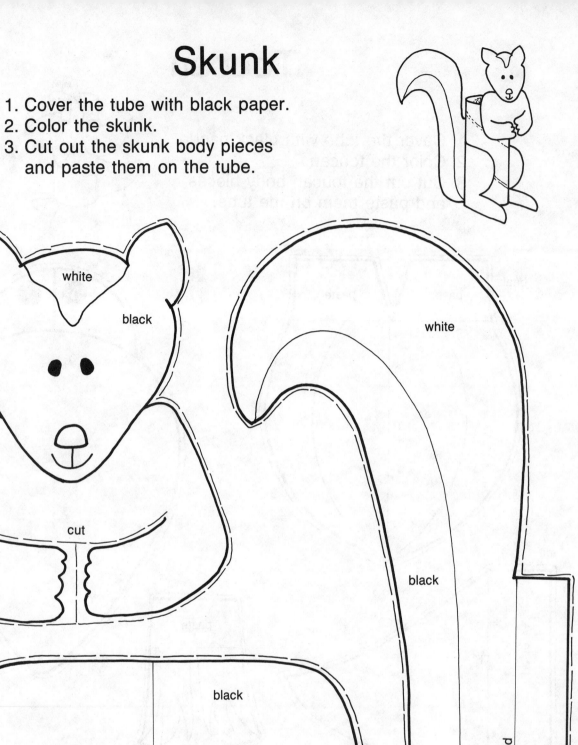

white

black

cut

black

fold

white

black

fold

paste

The Paper Tube Zoo

Crocodile

1. Cover the tube with green paper.
2. Color the crocodile.
3. Cut out the crocodile body pieces and paste them on the tube.

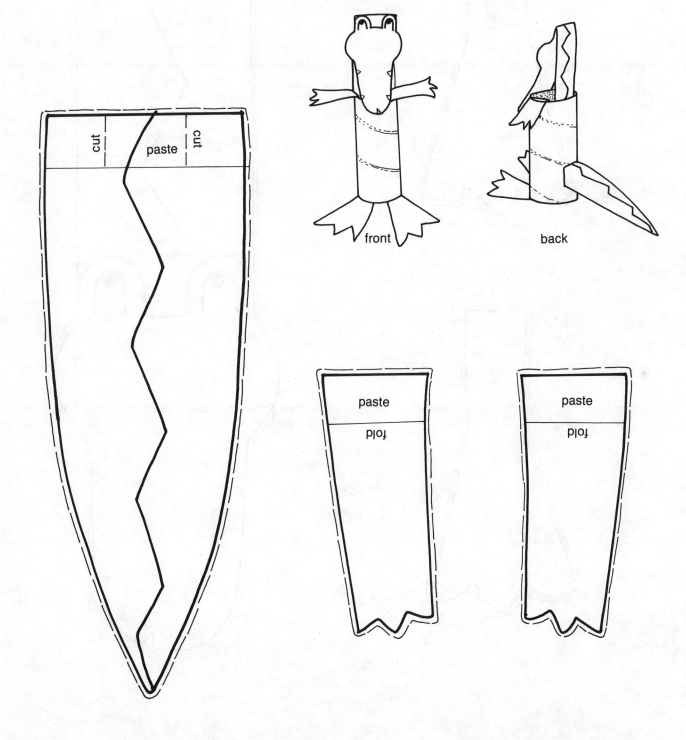

cut

paste

cut

front

back

paste

fold

paste

fold

The Paper Tube Zoo

Crocodile (continued)

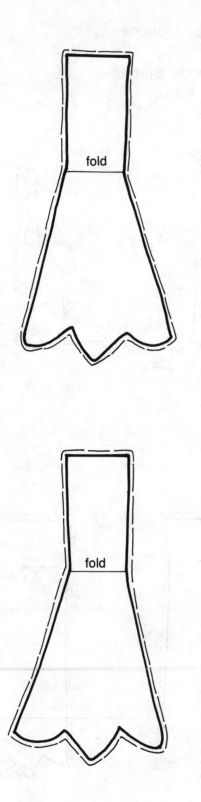

fold

fold

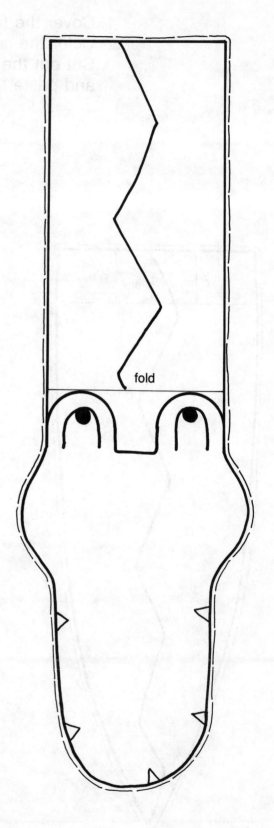

fold

22

Squirrel

1. Cover the tube with paper.
2. Color the squirrel.
3. Cut out the squirrel body pieces and paste them on the tube.

front   side

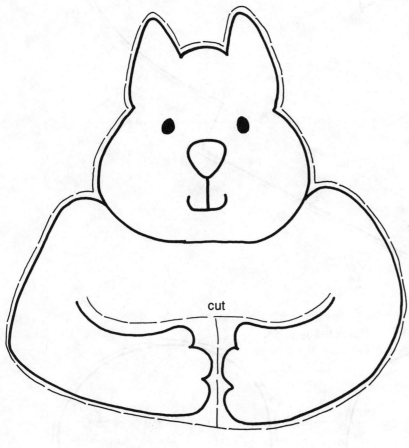

cut

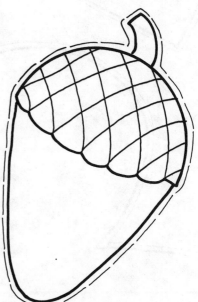

Paste the nut in squirrel's paws.

Squirrel (continued)

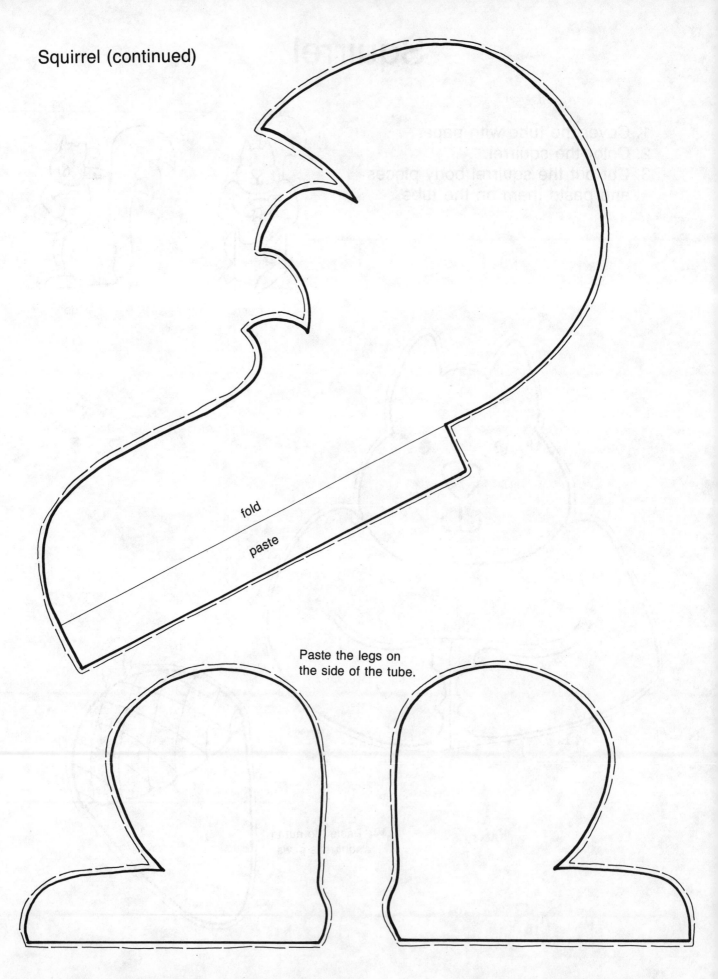

fold

paste

Paste the legs on
the side of the tube.

   The Paper Tube Zoo

Kangaroo

1. Cover the tube with brown paper.
2. Color the kangaroo and her baby.
3. Cut out the kangaroo body pieces and paste them on the tube.
4. Paste the baby inside the tube.

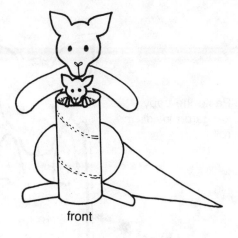

front

back

paste

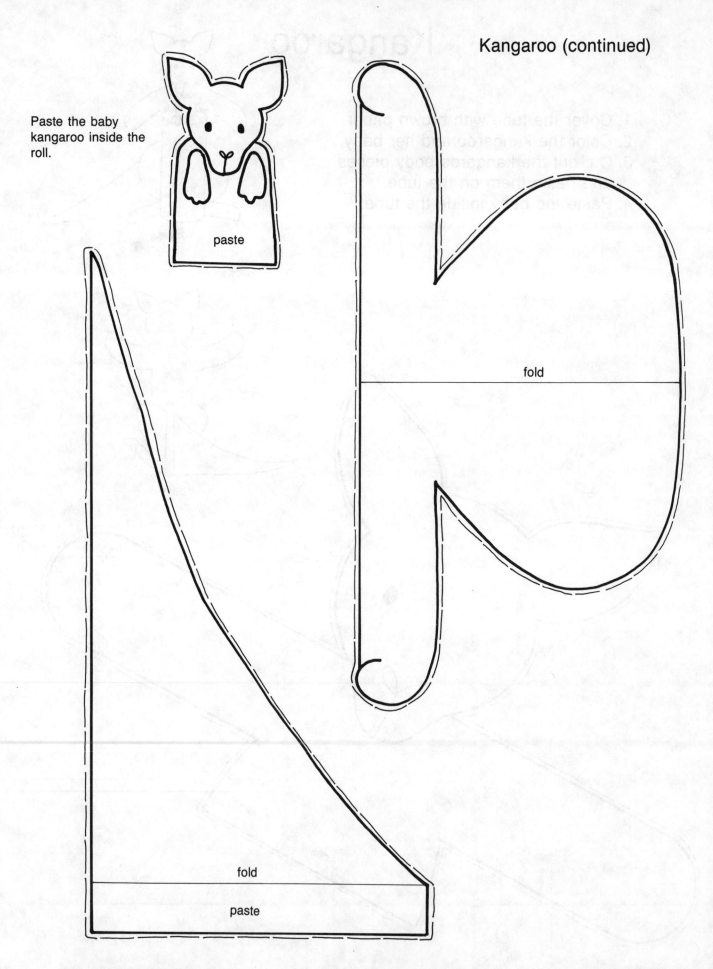

Paste the baby kangaroo inside the roll.

paste

fold

fold

paste

The Paper Tube Zoo

Elephant

1. Cover the tube with paper.
2. Color the elephant.
3. Cut out the elephant body pieces and paste them on the tube.

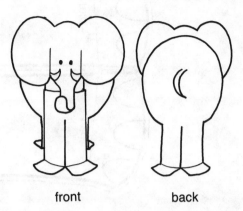

front   back

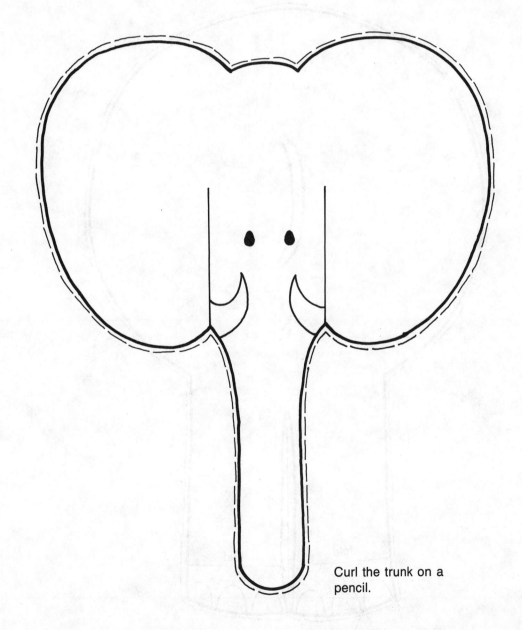

Curl the trunk on a pencil.

Elephant (continued)

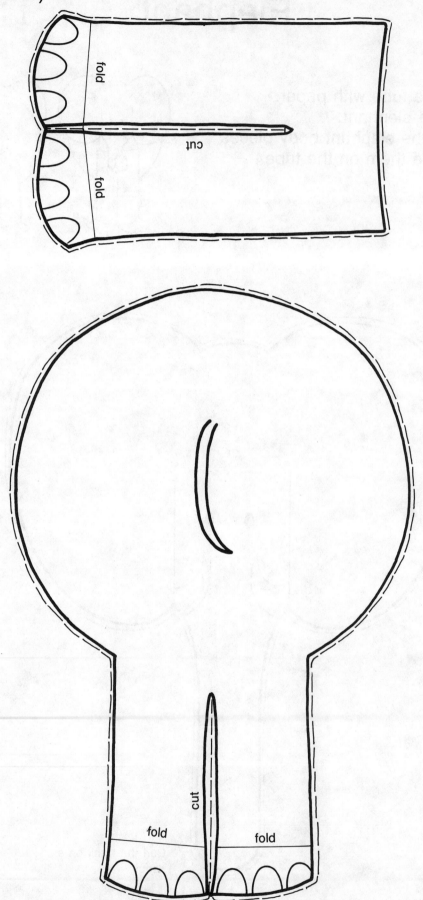

Giraffe

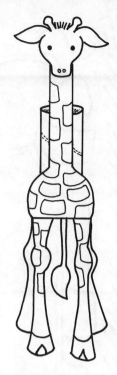

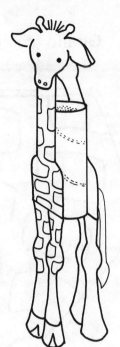

1. Cover the tube with yellow paper.
2. Color the giraffe.
3. Cut out the giraffe body pieces and paste them on the tube.

front

side

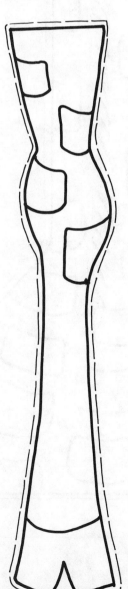

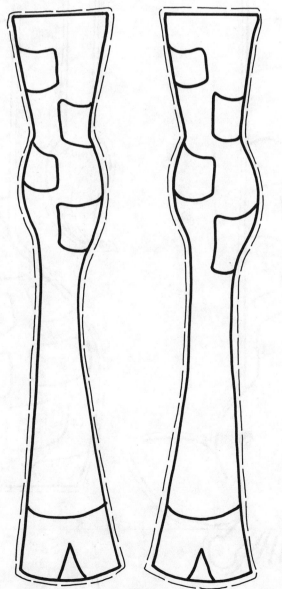

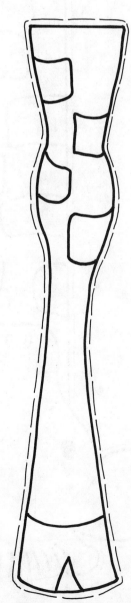

29

The Paper Tube Zoo

Giraffe (continued)

Paste the head
pieces together.

paste

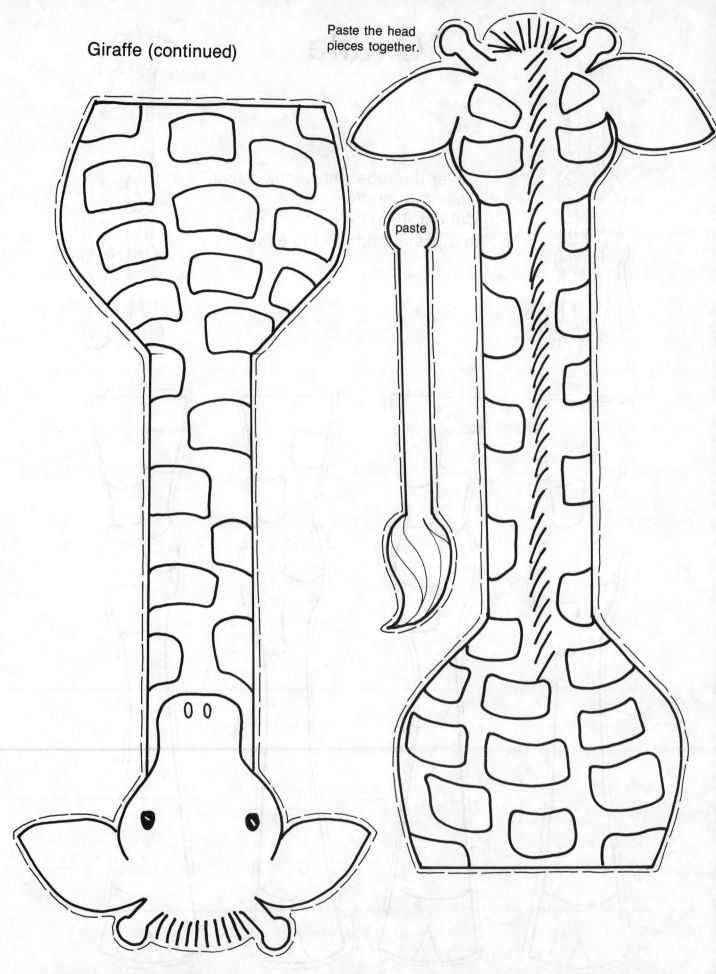

The Paper Tube Zoo

Dragon

1. Cover the tube with green paper.
2. Color the dragon.
3. Cut out the dragon pieces and
   paste them on the tube.

cut

31   The Paper Tube Zoo

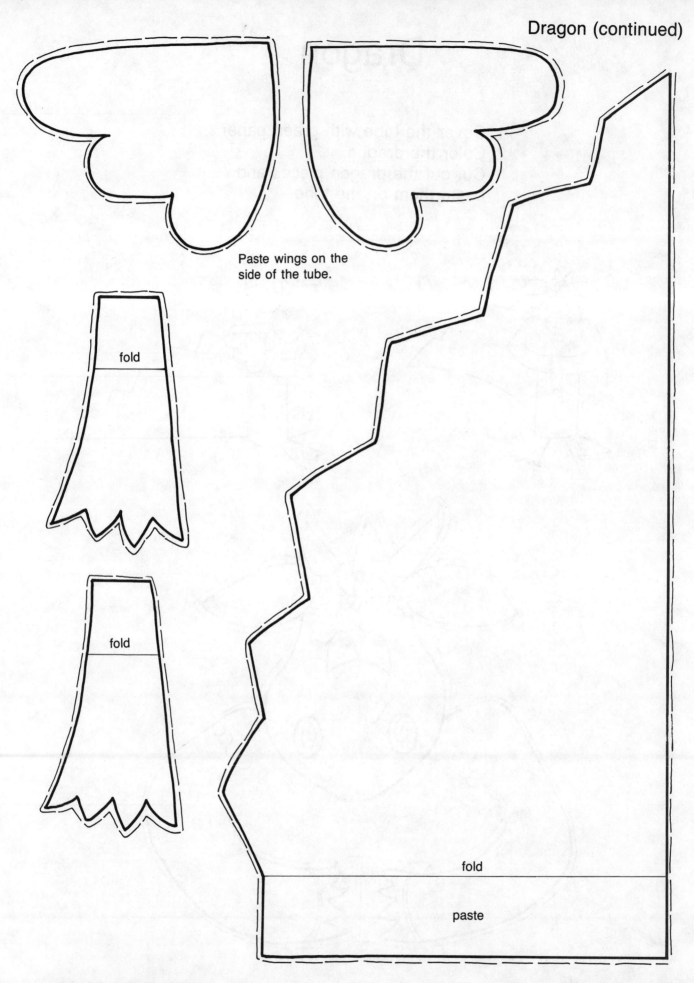

Paste wings on the
side of the tube.

fold

fold

fold

paste